Jazz Play Along

Book and CD for B♭, E♭ and C Instruments

Volume 13

John Coltrane

10 John Coltrane Classics

ISBN 978-0-634-05359-7

HAL•LEONARD®
CORPORATION

7777 W. BLUEMOUND RD. P.O. BOX 13819 MILWAUKEE, WI 53213

Visit Hal Leonard Online at
www.halleonard.com

John Coltrane

Arranged and Produced by
Mark Taylor

Featured Players:

Graham Breedlove-Trumpet
John Desalme-Tenor Sax
Tony Nalker-Piano
Jim Roberts-Bass
Steve Fidyk-Drums

HOW TO USE THE CD:

Each song has <u>two</u> tracks:

1) Split Track/Melody

Woodwind, Brass, Keyboard, and Mallet Players can use this track as a learning tool for melody style and inflection.

Bass Players can learn and perform with this track – remove the recorded bass track by turning down the volume on the LEFT channel.

Keyboard and **Guitar Players** can learn and perform with this track – remove the recorded piano part by turning down the volume on the RIGHT channel.

2) Full Stereo Track

Soloists or **groups** can learn and perform with this accompaniment track with the RHYTHM SECTION only.

BLUE TRAIN
BLUE TRANE

C VERSION

BY JOHN COLTRANE

COUNTDOWN

BY JOHN COLTRANE

C VERSION

CD
⬥5: SPLIT TRACK/MELODY
⬥6: FULL STEREO TRACK

COUSIN MARY

C VERSION

BY JOHN COLTRANE

EQUINOX

C VERSION

BY JOHN COLTRANE

GIANT STEPS

C VERSION

BY JOHN COLTRANE

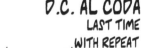

IMPRESSIONS

CD
11 : SPLIT TRACK/MELODY
12 : FULL STEREO TRACK

C VERSION

BY JOHN COLTRANE

LAZY BIRD

CD
13 : SPLIT TRACK/MELODY
14 : FULL STEREO TRACK

C VERSION

BY JOHN COLTRANE

CD
15 : SPLIT TRACK/MELODY
16 : FULL STEREO TRACK

MOMENT'S NOTICE

C VERSION

BY JOHN COLTRANE

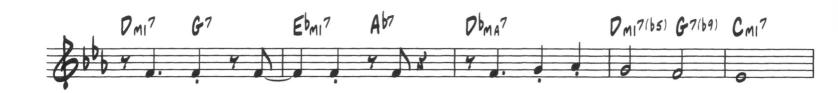

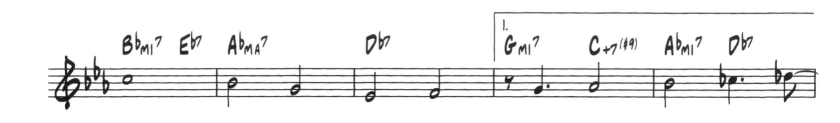

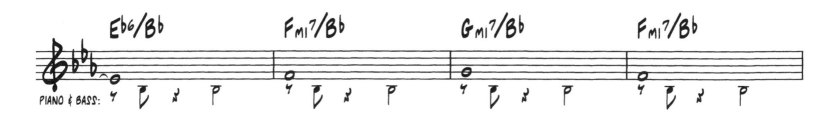

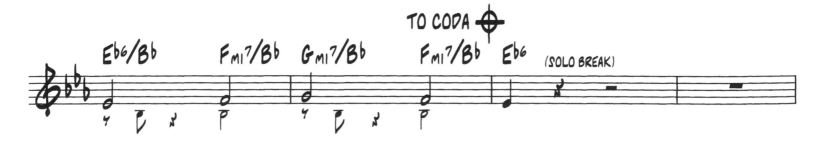

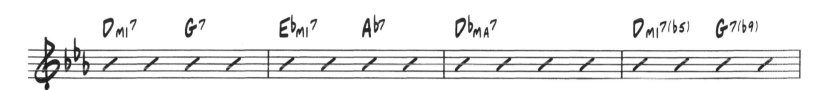

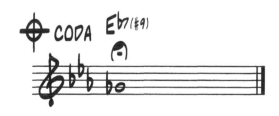

CD

17 : SPLIT TRACK/MELODY
18 : FULL STEREO TRACK

MR. P.C.

C VERSION

BY JOHN COLTRANE

NAIMA
NIEMA

BY JOHN COLTRANE

CD
◆19 : SPLIT TRACK/MELODY
◆20 : FULL STEREO TRACK

C VERSION

CD
① : SPLIT TRACK/MELODY
② : FULL STEREO TRACK

BLUE TRAIN
BLUE TRANE

B♭ VERSION

BY JOHN COLTRANE

COUNTDOWN

Bb VERSION

BY JOHN COLTRANE

COUSIN MARY

By JOHN COLTRANE

Bb VERSION

SWING

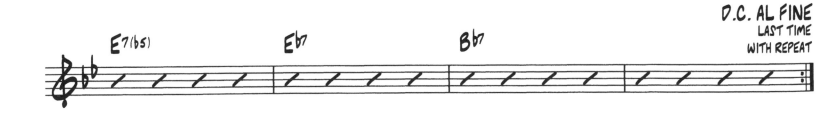

EQUINOX

CD
◆ 7 : SPLIT TRACK/MELODY
◆ 8 : FULL STEREO TRACK

Bb VERSION

BY JOHN COLTRANE

GIANT STEPS

Bb VERSION FAST SWING

BY JOHN COLTRANE

IMPRESSIONS

CD
⬦11: SPLIT TRACK/MELODY
⬦12: FULL STEREO TRACK

Bb VERSION

BY JOHN COLTRANE

LAZY BIRD

Bb VERSION

BY JOHN COLTRANE

MOMENT'S NOTICE

CD
15 : SPLIT TRACK/MELODY
16 : FULL STEREO TRACK

Bb VERSION

BY JOHN COLTRANE

MR. P.C.

BY JOHN COLTRANE

Bb VERSION

NAIMA
NIEMA

BY JOHN COLTRANE

Bb VERSION

CD
1: SPLIT TRACK/MELODY
2: FULL STEREO TRACK

BLUE TRAIN
BLUE TRANE

E♭ VERSION

BY JOHN COLTRANE

COUNTDOWN

COUSIN MARY

Eb VERSION

BY JOHN COLTRANE

EQUINOX

CD
⑦ : SPLIT TRACK/MELODY
◆ : FULL STEREO TRACK

Eb VERSION

BY JOHN COLTRANE

GIANT STEPS

Eb VERSION

BY JOHN COLTRANE

IMPRESSIONS

LAZY BIRD

Eᵇ VERSION

BY JOHN COLTRANE

MOMENT'S NOTICE

Eb VERSION

BY JOHN COLTRANE

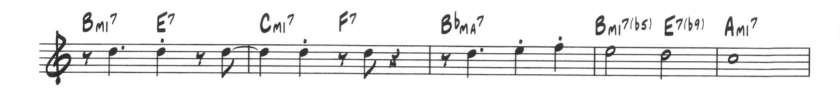

PIANO & BASS:

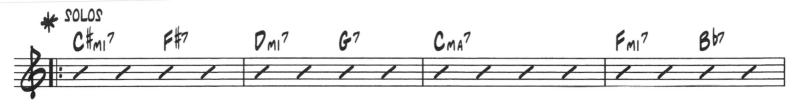

* SOLOS

C#mi7   F#7   Dmi7   G7   Cma7   Fmi7   Bb7

Bmi7   E7   Cmi7   F7   BbMa7   Bmi7(b5)   E7(b9)

Ami7   Gmi7   C7   Fma7   Bb7

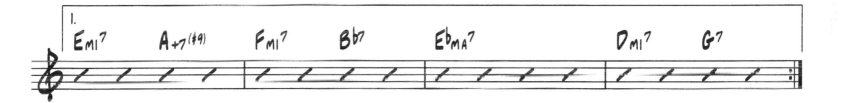

1.
Emi7   A+7(#9)   Fmi7   Bb7   EbMa7   Dmi7   G7

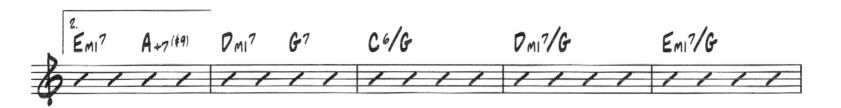

2.
Emi7   A+7(#9)   Dmi7   G7   C6/G   Dmi7/G   Emi7/G

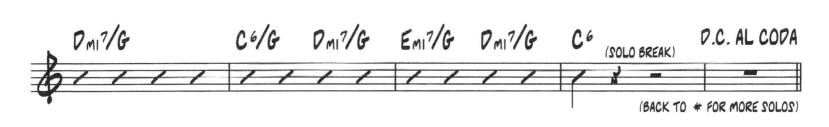

Dmi7/G   C6/G   Dmi7/G   Emi7/G   Dmi7/G   C6   (SOLO BREAK)   D.C. AL CODA

(BACK TO * FOR MORE SOLOS)

CODA
C7(#9)

MR. P.C.

BY JOHN COLTRANE

NAIMA
NIEMA

BY JOHN COLTRANE

BLUE TRAIN
BLUE TRANE

𝄢 C VERSION

BY JOHN COLTRANE

COUNTDOWN

BY JOHN COLTRANE

℗: C VERSION

COUSIN MARY

BY JOHN COLTRANE

♭: C VERSION

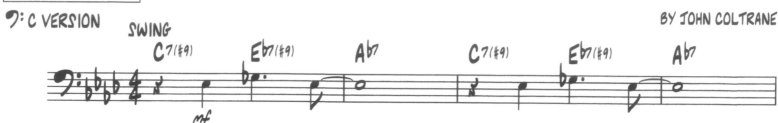

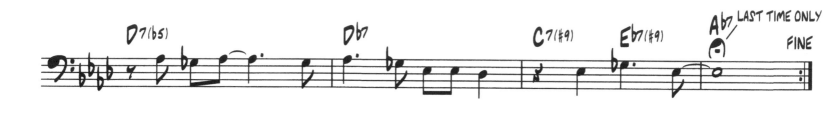

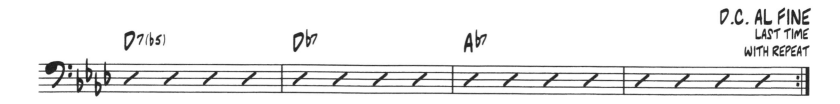

EQUINOX

CD
7 : SPLIT TRACK/MELODY
8 : FULL STEREO TRACK

BY JOHN COLTRANE

𝄢: C VERSION

Giant Steps

CD
◆9: SPLIT TRACK/MELODY
◆10: FULL STEREO TRACK

BY JOHN COLTRANE

𝄢: C VERSION

IMPRESSIONS

CD

13 : SPLIT TRACK/MELODY
14 : FULL STEREO TRACK

LAZY BIRD

BY JOHN COLTRANE

C VERSION   MEDIUM-UP SWING

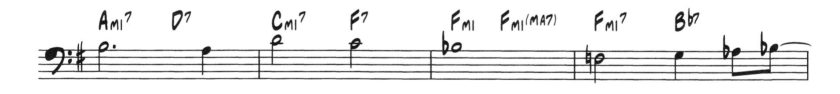

MOMENT'S NOTICE

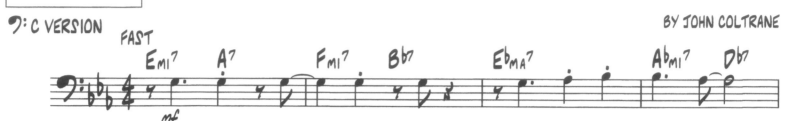

BY JOHN COLTRANE

: C VERSION

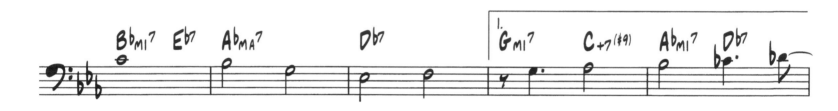

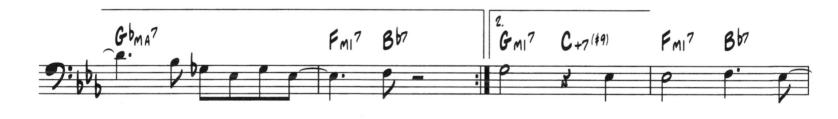

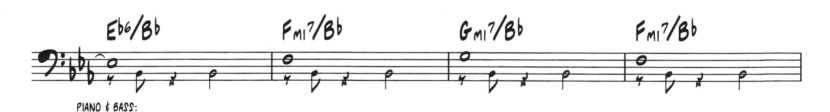

PIANO & BASS:

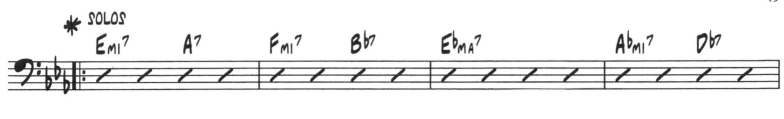

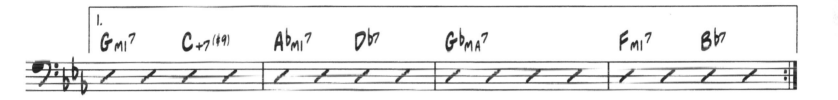

(BACK TO ✳ FOR MORE SOLOS)

MR. P.C.

BY JOHN COLTRANE

NAIMA
NIEMA

BY JOHN COLTRANE